"*Reset*"
Your Life

"*Reset*"
Your Life

Danielle Gonzalez

XULON PRESS

Xulon Press
2301 Lucien Way #415
Maitland, FL 32751
407.339.4217
www.xulonpress.com

Printed in the United States of America.

ISBN-13: 978-1-6312-9530-0
Ebook: 978-1-6312-9531-7

I am writing this book, with inspiration from God, as a practical guide to help others in need of hope, love, and the truth that sets us free. I first want to preface that if you haven't read *Battlefield of the Mind* by Joyce Meyer, please do so *immediately* after reading this book. She has an amazing story with a sound mind that will assist you with setting this book into motion.

Table of Contents

Chapter 1
Starting with the Basics

IF YOU ARE READING THIS BOOK, YOU ARE LOOKING for a reset (a re-do) at life. I know because I was there, too. I read books, manuals, and every Google article that I could find on happiness and moving forward, Until finally I just said, "God, you take over." That has been the best thing I have ever done!

First, if you don't know God, let's start there. God gave us the Bible as a way to show us how to live our lives (first written somewhere between 1200 and 1450 BC). Over the years, it has been translated into many languages and dialects to make it easier for us to grasp, based on where we live and the language we speak. It's not difficult—it was just written in a different time, and we must understand that part first. I personally like "The New Living Translation" (NLT), "The Passion Translation" (TPT), and "The New International Version" (NIV) as they take all the *thee's* and *thy's* out, and are fairly simple in their context. However, the key is finding one that is comfortable for you!

What we know about the Bible: it was written in two parts (sixty-six individual books written by different people over a period of about 1600 years, and then put together): the Old Testament (written in Hebrew), and the New Testament (written in Greek). The Old Testament starts with the creation of Earth in Genesis, but also contains a history of great heroes and prophets of the day. Stories of Noah, Abraham, Moses, Samson, Esther, Elijah, and David are all good to read and study to understand how God worked through them to help the people of the day. It also talks about things that will happen in the future (the future for that time; many of the predictions have already taken place!). In those days, God spoke to people through high priests and prophets, through dreams, and through the Tabernacle, a sacred place built by men according to the instruction of God (Ex. 25-40). God spoke (sometimes by way of a cloud, through fire, or with His voice) only to the high priests and to the holiest men of God in the Tabernacle, using these people to communicate His instructions to the people on how to live out their lives. Blood sacrifices (of animals) were also key in the forgiveness of sins. Each type of sin required a different type of pure and holy sacrifice to cleanse the person/people of their sins. This, in turn, was the way into heaven… then.

Fast-forward to the New Testament, first written about 60 AD. Jesus came into the world and onto the scene. He was born of a virgin (the Virgin Mary) and she was to marry Joseph (a carpenter). Matthew, Mark, Luke, and John are the first four authors who write the story of Jesus and His disciples from each of their perspectives. If you have not read any of the Bible yet, please <u>read these 4 books first</u>. They will help you to understand how powerful Jesus was (and is) and what His purpose was for leaving His heavenly home to come down to Earth to save each one of us! Yes, God has a purpose for each of us! The goal of Jesus's disciples was to be witnesses to His life, and to tell people of the miracles and all the wonderful things that He did while here on Earth. Things no one else did before and no one will do again until He returns. They were to share the news and document it for the rest of humanity. He was their Lord, the Son of God, now seated at the Right Hand of God to perfect the Trinity (Father, Son, and Holy Spirit). He only dwelled on Earth for thirty to thirty-five short years before sacrificing His life for our sins and being resurrected three days later.

This was God's way of changing the dynamics of HOW people got to Heaven. Jesus IS the holiest of blood sacrifices. Through Him is now how we get to God and heaven—no more sacrificing of animals for the forgiveness of our sins or having to go through a high priest to speak to Him. Isn't this great news? You can speak directly to God anytime you want!

If you have never asked God to forgive your sins, so you know that you will be with Him forever, now would be a good time. Pray something like this: "Lord, I believe that you are the Son of God. I believe that you died on the cross as the sacrifice for my sins. I know that by nature, I am a sinner, and I ask you now to come into my heart, cleanse me of my sins, and allow me to be with you, in heaven, forever. Amen."

Continuing along in the New Testament, you'll find some more witnesses of Jesus and His life. Paul (another amazing Bible hero) writes thirteen letters to the seven churches, along with many other books of the New Testament. Several of Jesus's disciples, including James (the actual half-brother of Jesus), write more of the books, continuing to share the news of the Lord.

Revelation, the last and final book of the Bible, tells us what the future holds for Earth and the people who are still here in the last days. There you have it in the extremely condensed version; life from the beginning of human existence to the end, with God the Father, who says, "I am the Alpha and the Omega, the First and the Last, the Beginning and the End" (Rev. 22:13, NIV).

The rest of the New Testament is a "how-to" guide for life: how to live life according to what God has planned for you here on Earth, how to love others, how to get to know that third part of the Trinity (the Holy Spirit), how to have faith, how to live by faith, how to renew our minds and spirits, how to live a life that is worthy in His eyes, and how to tap into that power that only God can supply. This is where we begin!

Chapter 2
Moving Forward–
Transform Your Mind

ROMANS 12:1-2 SAYS: "AND SO, DEAR BROTHERS AND sisters, [Paul talking to the Roman church] I plead with you to give your bodies to God because of all he has done for you. Let them be a living and holy sacrifice-the kind he will find acceptable. This is truly the way to worship him. Don't copy the behavior and customs of this world, but let God transform you into a new person by changing the **way you think**. Then you will learn to know God's will for you, which is good and pleasing and perfect."(NLT)

For years I was "playing the recording" over and over again in my head of how things could have gone so awry; how a marriage ended so early with two little children, and all the things we could have done, or not done, to make this happen. I struggled to forgive myself, but God understood and forgave me. All I had to do was ask. He had to change my thinking first, starting in my mind.

> "Study this book of Instruction continually. Meditate on it day and night so you will be sure to obey everything written in it. Only then will you prosper and succeed in all you do. This is my command – be strong and courageous! Do not be afraid or discouraged. For the Lord your God is with you wherever you go." (Joshua 1:8-9, NLT)

The Bible is God's Word; it is His instruction manual for life. It will speak to you if you let it. Sometimes, I will read one passage and not really think too much on it. Then, at a later time, I will read it again, and the words will just come off the page and an understanding will set it. I know I have read it before, but this time it "speaks" to me. God speaks to me. In order to transform your mind, you have to start reading and start understanding how God thinks. Then He will help you to understand your life and your purpose more clearly.

> You were taught, with regard to your former way of life, to put off your old self, which is being corrupted by its deceitful desires; to be made new in the attitude of your minds; And to put on the new self, created to be like God in true righteousness and holiness. (Ephesians 4:22-24, NIV)

Don't keep "playing the recording" over and over again in your head. Repent, forgive (yourself and others), let it go, and move forward. Move forward in your "new self." Pray that God will show you what He has planned, to reveal His will for your life.

Apparently I am writing a book. Have I ever done this before? No! But one day, in prayer, I got a very specific and deliberate word upon my heart to write a book, so here I am! What a change of direction for me. I haven't written a paper since college over twenty years ago, let alone a book. He is leading me in a direction that I would have never thought of on my own. How exciting it is!

Chapter 3
Transform Your Heart

PROVERBS 4:20-23 (WRITTEN BY SOLOMON) SAYS: "MY child, pay attention to what I say. Listen carefully to my words. Don't lose sight of them. Let them penetrate deep into your heart, for they bring life to those who find them, and healing to their whole body. Guard your heart above all else, for it determines the course of your life." (NLT)

If you do this, you will refocus your mind according to your heart. This will be the healing you need— healing from the inside out. Healing that only God can provide. Look within and pray for yourself to be made whole.

When I was younger (much younger—fifteen, specifically), I met a boy at "church camp." I was "in love." We lived in Florida and he lived on the the other side of the state. We planned to meet at Disney's "Night of Joy," which was an annual Christian concert that Disney World in Orlando, Florida put on each year, featuring multiple bands. I drove to Orlando with a few of my friends from youth group, and he went with his youth group on a bus; we planned to meet in front of Space Mountain. Now this is going back a while— prior to cell phones. I know, I am dating myself here... but we actually had to use a phone with a cord that was stuck to a wall! So, when we left for the trip, there was no talking to him until we met up at the location we had agreed upon. Several of us planned to stay at a friend's house that evening and drive back home the next day. We got to the parks, and it was total excitement with all the people coming and going. We headed to the entrance of Space Mountain and we waited... and waited... and waited.

We walked around in circles and looked everywhere. My heart sank, and I sensed that something was very wrong. I didn't just know... I *knew*. I felt it. I was in hysterics by 8 PM and I didn't even know why!

We continued through the night and went back to the friend's house as planned. We woke up in the morning to hear the terrible news that came at breakfast: their bus never made it to the parks that day. They pulled over on the side of the highway when their bus got a flat tire, and the passengers exited the bus while the tire was being changed. Another driver came along, who had been drinking too much, and hit the rear of the bus; they spun into the kids who were waiting on the side of the road. Five were killed instantly and many others injured. He was one of the five.

When I tell you that I was devastated, I could not even breathe. I could not understand, at that age (or any age, for that matter), why something like that could happen. I was hurt; I was sad for all their families; and then... I was mad. I was mad at myself for making the plans to meet him, because, in my head, then it would never have happened. I was mad that I couldn't change it. And then, I was mad at God for letting it happen. I was mad at Him for *many* years. What I did not realize was that I couldn't see the things God had planned. Things like that are not orchestrated by God. There are spirits in this world that are at work all the time, trying to undo all the good that God has planned. God was not the one to blame, but we, being human, feel the need to always blame someone. So, what do we do? We blame Him.

He is with God, and I know that now. And one day I will see him again. Don't do what I did! Don't waste time being mad at God for things that happen in life. Things will happen, people will get hurt, storms in life will come, and loved ones will be lost in this life. Know that if they believe, you will be with them again! Recognize and change the pattern NOW! Change it before you lose all that time living with heartache and regret instead of understanding the truth and letting Him help you through it.

Pray. Pray all day, every day. Pray while you are driving, stuck in traffic, while you are at work, while you are in the shower, while you are cleaning the house, and before bed. It does not have to be weird— speak from your heart like you are talking to a friend. He already knows what is in your heart anyway!

If you are believing for something specific, pray that it is in His will. If it is, you will be blessed with it. If not, then you need to move forward and ask God to change your heart and give you wisdom and understanding to know what is in His plan for you. In Matthew 7:7-8, Jesus speaks regarding prayer and how we should pray. "Ask, and the gift is yours. Seek, and the door will be opened for you. For every persistent one will get what he asks for. And everyone who knocks persistently will one day find an open door." (TPT) Open the door to your heart and mind!

Jesus's message and prayer for us!

In John 17, Jesus is praying to God regarding His disciples, right before He is betrayed, arrested and taken to the cross. He says, starting in verse 9:

> My prayer is not for the world, but for those you have given me, because they belong to you. All who are mine belong to you, and you have given them to me, so they bring me glory. Now I am departing from the world; they are staying in this world, but I am coming to you. Holy Father,

you have given me your name, now protect them by the power of your name so that they will be united just as we are. During my time here, I protected them by the power of the name you gave me. I guarded them so that not one was lost, except the one headed for destruction, as the Scriptures foretold."(Speaking of Judas— the disciple who betrayed Jesus). "Now I am coming to you. I told them many things while I was with them in this world so they would be filled with my joy. I have given them your word. And the world hates them because they do not belong to the world, just as I do not belong to the world. I'm not asking you to take them out of the world, but to keep them safe from the evil one. They do not belong to this world any more than I do. Make them holy by your truth; teach them your word, which is truth. Just as you sent me into the world, I am sending them into the world. **And I give myself as a holy sacrifice for them so they can be made holy by your truth. I am praying not only for these disciples but also for all who will ever believe in me through their message. I pray that they will all be one, just as you and I are one—as you are in me, Father, and I am in you. And may they be in us so that the world will believe you sent me.**" (NLT)

Wow! So much going on here—so much revealed! First of all, if you don't already know, there is a heaven and there is a hell. Real places, not symbols for some strange phenomenon. There is evil in this world that Jesus wants to protect His disciples from. But He is not just praying for protection for His disciples; He is praying for "all who will ever believe in me through their message." That is us! Thank you, Lord, for protecting us!

He wants us to know Him, to believe in Him, and ultimately, to be with Him forever. Once you grasp this, you can move forward to the next wonderful step He has planned for us.

Chapter 4
The Holy Spirit

JOHN 14:25-29 STARTS WITH JESUS SPEAKING WITH HIS disciples. He says: "I am telling you these things now while I am still with you. But when the Father sends the Advocate as my representative—that is, the Holy Spirit—He will teach you everything and will remind you of everything I have told you. I am leaving you with a gift—peace of mind and heart. And the peace I give is a gift the world cannot give. So, don't be troubled or afraid. I have told you these things before they happen so that when they do happen, you will believe." (NLT)

The Holy Spirit is the third portion of that Trinity we talked about earlier (Father, Son, and Holy Spirit). He is just that: a spirit. He is with us all the time and speaks to us in the form of that tiny little voice inside our very being. The one that knows us better than anyone in the whole world. Why? Because He is God. But, unfortunately, most of the time, we don't listen to Him. I know I didn't. Oh, I heard Him alright, and I felt Him, but I let other voices drown out the voice that was in my heart. The voice in my head took over and it was a battle of wills. I knew I should be listening to one voice (thinking back on it now), but made a clear decision <u>NOT</u> to listen to the voice of my heart. Have you ever felt yourself going around and around in circles and never getting anywhere? That was me! That decision (or indecision) literally got me nowhere—just many years of wasted time.

Romans 8:5-14 talks about the Holy Spirit and, more specifically, what is in store for the people who embrace Him. This again is Paul speaking to the Roman church: "Those who are motivated by the flesh only pursue what benefits themselves. But those who live by the impulses of the Holy Spirit are motivated to pursue spiritual realities. For the mind-set of the flesh is death, but the mind-set controlled by the Spirit finds life and peace." (TPT)

Peace—isn't that what we all want? PEACE...
internal PEACE!

Continuing on later with verse twelve: "Therefore, dear brothers and sisters, you have no obligation to do what your sinful nature urges you to do. For if you live by its dictates, you will die. But if through the power of the Spirit you put to death the deeds of your sinful nature, you will live. For all who are led by the Spirit of God are children of God." (NLT)

So, from my understanding, **we choose**. We choose to listen to the Spirit, or not, which determines the path our lives will take. It's as simple as that. We choose to accept Him; to let Him into our lives. He freely gives the choice to all of us by His grace. It is our job to make the decision to accept it. If you want to reset your life, choose to listen to the Spirit. Choose to move forward in the path God has already set for you. God sets it, the Spirit helps it to move along in the direction it should go. Then, we will have His peace in our lives and can live as His children. An innocent child doesn't think about their actions prior to acting. They just feel something and go with it. That is what makes them innocent. That is how we should act. Not foolishly, but with Godly wisdom. Act innocently, but not immaturely. There is a difference! True wisdom comes from God.

For wherever there is jealousy and selfish ambition, there you will find disorder and evil of every kind. But the wisdom from above is

first of all pure. It is also peace loving, gentle
at all times, and willing to yield to others. It
is full of mercy and good deeds. It shows no
favoritism and is always sincere.. And those
who are peacemakers will plant seeds of peace
and reap a harvest of righteousness. (James
3:16-18 NLT)

How wonderful it is to know that we have a father that
is good—a father that will guide us with wisdom if we let
Him, and a father that loves His children so much that He
seeks that not any go astray. We see this clearly explained in
the "Parable of the Lost Sheep" (Luke 15:4-7): "There once
was a shepherd with a hundred lambs, but one of his lambs
wandered away and was lost. So the shepherd left the ninety-
nine lambs out in the open field and searched in the wilderness
for that one lost lamb. He didn't stop until he finally found
it. With exuberant joy he raised it up and placed it on his
shoulders, carrying it back with cheerful delight! Returning
home, he called all his friends and neighbors together and said,
Let's have a party! Come and celebrate with me the return of
my lost lamb. It wandered away, but I found it and bought
it home.'" Jesus continued, "In the same way, there will be
a glorious celebration in heaven over the rescue of one lost
sinner who repents, comes back home, and returns to the
fold—more so than for all the righteous people who never
strayed away.'"" (TPT)

He wants us all to "choose" to follow Him.

Once you choose to do this, trust God to step in. **God protects His children**. "The Lord directs the steps of the godly. He delights inn every detail of their lives. Though they stumble, they will never fall, for the Lord holds them by the hand" (Psalm 37:23-24 NLT).

God gives us promises that He is with us and will never leave us. "Trust in the Lord with all your heart; do not depend on your own understanding. Seek his will in all you do, and he will show you which path to take" (Prov. 3:5-6 NLT).

He gave the same promises to the people of the Old Testament. When Joshua becomes the leader of the Israelites, Moses tells him: "The LORD himself goes before you and will be with you; he will never leave you nor forsake you. Do not be afraid; do not be discouraged." (Deuteronomy 31:8 NIV).

The Lord is with us always. We need to remember this and carry out our lives with this knowledge and reverence. We need to let the Spirit lead us.

But the fruit produced by the Holy Spirit within you is divine love in all its varied expressions:

joy *that overflows,*
peace *that subdues,*
patience *that endures,*
kindness *in action,*
a life full of virtue,
faith *that prevails,*
gentleness *of heart, and*
strength *of spirit.*

Never set the law above these qualities, for they are meant to be limitless. (Galatians 5:22-23 TPT)

For those that choose to take this to the next level, there is a heavenly language that only God can give. We call it speaking in "tongues" or speaking in the Spirit. But, really, it is your heart (spirit) communing directly with the Spirit of God.

> And the Holy Spirit helps us in our weakness. For example, we don't know what God wants us to pray for. But the Holy Spirit prays for us with groanings that cannot be expressed in words. And the Father who knows all hearts knows what the Spirit is saying, for the Spirit pleads for us believers in harmony with God's own will. And we know that God causes everything to work together for the good of those who love God and are called according to his purpose for them. (Romans 8: 26-28 NLT)

I could write a whole another book on this. But for now, just know that this is available to anyone who is saved (who believes in Jesus), and it will be given if you ask Him for it. You can read more about the Spiritual Gifts in 1 Corinthians, chapters 12-14.

Chapter 5
A New Perspective, A New Direction

PAUL WROTE MANY OF THE BOOKS OF THE NEW Testament while in prison in Rome. In one of his letters to the people in Philippi, he wrote: "No, dear brothers and sisters, I have not achieved it [speaking of perfection], but I focus on this one thing; Forgetting the past and looking forward to what lies ahead, I press on to reach the end of the race and receive the heavenly prize for which God, through Christ Jesus, is calling us. (Philippians 3:13-14 NLT).

Here we see that we will never be perfect. Sometimes I ask for forgiveness for the same things over and over again. But God knows our nature and understands us fully. He wants us to put the past behind us and move forward in Him. He does not want us to become tired and weary, although sometimes it does require patience. Remember that God's timing is not always our timing. He sees the whole picture when we can just see a little bit at a time.

> The Lord is my shepherd, I shall not be in want. He makes me lie down in green pastures, he leads me beside quiet waters, he restores my soul. He guides me in paths of righteousness for his name's sake. Even though I walk through the valley of the shadow of death, I will fear no evil, for you are with me; your rod and your staff, they comfort me." (Psalm 23:1-4 NIV)

Although this verse is used for many purposes, the context is more of a comfort for the ones going through storms. Storms are a part of life and will continue to come. It is how we handle ourselves in the middle of those storms that will get us through. Knowing that God will "hold our hand" through the storms is key! If we have faith, we can get through every storm and not be afraid.

Proverbs 3: 21-24 says, "My child, never drift off course from these two goals for your life: to walk in wisdom and to discover discernment. Don't ever forget how they empower you. For they strengthen you inside and out and inspire you to do what's right; you will be energized and refreshed by the healing they bring. They give you living hope to guide you, and not one of life's tests will cause you to stumble. You will sleep like a baby, safe and sound – your rest will be sweet and secure." (TPT) Here we can see that we are protected, and we need not be afraid. No matter what happens in life, we need to look to God for wisdom and use good judgement.

Matthew 8:23-27 speaks about what happened to Jesus when He was with His disciples on the water. "Then Jesus got into the boat and started across the lake with his disciples. Suddenly, a fierce storm struck the lake, with waves breaking into the boat. But Jesus was sleeping. The disciples went and woke him up, shouting, 'Lord, save us! We're going to drown!' Jesus responded, 'Why are you afraid? You have so little faith!' Then he got up and rebuked the wind and waves, and suddenly there was a great calm. The disciples were amazed. 'Who is this man?' They asked. 'Even the winds and waves obey him!'" (NLT) This is a literal example of a storm, but the principal is the same. If we have faith, Jesus will get us through the storms of life and give us a calming peace! Don't you think that if He can calm the wind and waves, He can certainly calm any storm you are going through (or at least calm our perspective of the storm while we are in it)?

God is our refuge and strength, always ready
to help in times of trouble. So we will not fear
when earthquakes come and the mountains
crumble into the sea. (Psalm 46:1-2 NLT)

Look within, pray for yourself to be made whole, pray
for wisdom and understanding, pray for God's will for your
life. Understand that trials and tribulations will come, but
you can overcome them with the help of God. Leave the past
behind you and move forward knowing and trusting that God
will take care of you no matter what you are going through
(or have gone through). Let Him be the one you look to for
guidance, understanding and peace. No one on this earth can
give that. He must be your source!

Chapter 6
Freedom

IF YOU GET THE CHANCE TO TAKE A FREEDOM CLASS, I highly encourage you to do so. It is offered as a small group at some churches by Highlands. It is a game changer—a fresh way to let go of all you have been carrying and give it to God. We carry so much weight in and throughout our lives, and we were never made to do that. That wasn't the life that God intended us to live. We worry about everything and live as if we have nothing, when really we have an incredible amount to be thankful for. We need to start thanking Him every day and not continue to be burdened in that same manner.

> Then, "Jesus taught his disciples, saying, 'Listen to me. Never let anxiety enter your hearts. Never worry about any of your needs, such as food or clothing. For your life is infinitely more than just food or the clothing you wear. Take the carefree birds as your example. Do you ever see them worry? They don't grow their own food or put it in a storehouse for later. Yet God takes care of every one of them, feeding each of them from his love and goodness. Isn't your life more precious to God than a bird? *Be carefree in the care of God!*'" (Luke 12:22-26 TPT)

Here we see that the worry we carry is not necessary nor productive in any way. This is NOT the way to freedom. We have to give it to God. Let Him help you. Let Him hold you by the hand and carry your burdens for you. Ask Him for what it is that you want, and, if it is in His will, it will be provided to you.

All of this is for your benefit. And as God's grace reaches more and more people, there will be great thanksgiving, and God will receive more and more glory. That is why we never give up. Though our bodies are dying, our spirits are being renewed every day.. For our present troubles are small and won't last very long. Yet they produce for us a glory that vastly outweighs them and will last forever! So we don't look at the troubles we can see now; rather, we fix our gaze on things that cannot be seen. For the things we see now will soon be gone, but the things we cannot see will last forever. (2 Corinthians 4:15-18, NLT)

Jesus is the way to freedom. Remember how earlier we talked about the "Old Testament way of life"? Well, this is the New Testament way of life; when Jesus was hanging on the cross, He paved the way for us to live in a new way with God.

In Matthew 27:45-52 we read: "At noon, darkness fell across the whole land until three o'clock. At about three o'clock, Jesus called out with a loud voice, 'Eli, Eli, lema sabachthani?' Which means My God, my God, why have you abandoned me? … Then Jesus shouted out again, and he released His spirit. At that moment the curtain in the sanctuary of the Temple was torn in two, from top to bottom. The earth shook, rocks split apart, and tombs opened." Everyone there believed that He was the Son of God after that; even the Roman soldiers were terrified by the experience and stated in verse 54, "This man truly was the Son of God!" (NLT)

This account shows us the price that Jesus paid for us, and the "new way" to God. The curtain in the temple symbolizes God ending the "old way" and beginning this new way of entering into God's kingdom, through Jesus.

In 2 Corinthians 3:16-17, we see that the curtain, the veil, was torn in the Temple (or Tabernacle, which we mentioned earlier) at that exact time that Jesus released His Spirit. When the veil is taken away, then there is freedom. "But the moment one turns to the Lord with an open heart, the veil is lifted *and they see.* Now, the 'Lord' *I'm referring to* is the Holy Spirit, and wherever he is Lord, there is freedom." (TPT)

Be Free!

Chapter 7
Trust in Him

No MATTER WHAT HAPPENS EACH DAY, LOOK TO GOD for your hope, look to Him for your purpose, and look to Him for your instruction. Do not do anything without consulting Him. He will let you know which direction to go, who to have relationships with, what to do, and who to pray for. Trust in what He says and do *not go your own way*! If we are perfectly honest, that is what led us to where we are in the first place— yes all of us; myself included! How many years I have wasted just going my own way!

> **Trust in the Lord with all your heart; do not depend on your own understanding. Seek his will in all you do, and he will show you which path to take.** (Proverbs 3:5-6 NLT)

It may not make any sense in your mind, but trust God to lead you in the path that was ultimately designed for you from the beginning. Sometimes we take detours (sometimes very long detours), but regardless, you are on the right track now. Do not let anyone influence you. Always consult with the Lord for direction, despite what your flesh (your mind) may want. We are weak, but He is strong. He will guide us and hold us if we need to be held. Always remember that He will never give us something too big for us to handle. It may not feel like it, but you will come out victorious!

Paul, speaking to the church of Ephesus in Ephesians 3:14-19, says,:"When I think of all this, I fall to my knees and pray to the Father, the Creator of everything in heaven and on earth. I pray that from his glorious, unlimited resources he will empower you with inner strength through his Spirit. Then Christ will make his home in your hearts as you trust in him. Your roots will grow down into God's love and keep you strong. **And may you have the power to understand, as all God's people should, how wide, how long, how high, and how deep his love is. May you experience the love of Christ, though it is too great to understand fully. Then you will be made complete with all the fullness of life and power that comes from God."** (NLT)

I pray for you to have faith and trust in the Lord. No matter what circumstances may bring, put your trust in Him. For He is in control and although we have no concept or understanding of what this looks like, that is what FAITH is. The foundation of His incomprehensible love is what we lean on to bring us through. Be thankful for it, as every day is a new day in His eyes. We need to remember that with each new day-when the sun is starting to peak over the horizon, and the birds are happily chirping in the branches, that it is a new day for us too!

> As for us, we have all of these great witnesses who encircle us like clouds. So we must let go of every wound that has pierced us and the sin we so easily fall into. Then we will be able to run life's marathon race with passion and determination, for the path has been already marked out before us. We look away from the natural realm and we fasten our gaze onto Jesus who birthed faith within us and who leads us forward into faith's perfection. His example is this: Because his heart was focused on the joy of knowing that you would be his, he endured the agony of the cross and conquered its humiliation, and now sits exalted at the right

hand of the throne of God! So consider carefully how Jesus faced such intense opposition from sinners who opposed their own souls, so that you won't become worn down and cave in under life's pressures." (Hebrews 12:1-3 TPT)

Jesus was the only one who never sinned on earth. He did this so we could have life. His was the purest sacrifice. He was tempted in every way, the same as you and I. But so that every Scripture was fulfilled, He did not falter.

> We can make our own plans, but the Lord gives the right answer. People may be pure in their own eyes, but the Lord examines their motives. Commit your actions to the Lord, and your plans will succeed. The Lord has made everything for his own purposes, even the wicked for a day of disaster. (Proverbs 16:1-4 NLT)

As we think about each new day, try to remember that you are in control of your thoughts and emotions. Keep your motives for doing things in check. Let your heart guide you and then proceed in that direction, otherwise you are working against God. If we go our own way, even for [what seems like] the small things, we are not relying on His direction.

Psalm 91:1-4 says, "He who dwells in the shelter of the Most High will rest in the shadow of he Almighty. I will say of the LORD, 'He is my refuge and my fortress, my God, in whom I trust.' Surely he will save you from the fowler's snare and from the deadly pestilence. **He will cover you with his**

feathers, and under his wings you will find refuge; his faithfulness will be your shield and rampart." (NIV)

I don't know about you, but I want to sleep cuddled up underneath God's wings! When we put our trust in Him, we give our control over to Him. We surrender our will and put His in the forefront of our life. When we do this, He not only guides us, He becomes our Protector. He will protect us from every harm and every evil thing.

> If you make the Most High your dwelling—even the LORD, who is my refuge—then no harm will befall you, no disaster will come near your tent. For he will command his angels concerning you to guard you in all your ways; they will lift you up in their hands, so that you will not strike your foot against a stone. You will tread upon the lion and the cobra; you will trample the great lion and the serpent. 'Because he loves me,' says the LORD, I will rescue him; I will protect him, for he acknowledges my name. (Psalm 91:9-14 NIV)

Who doesn't want God's angels protecting them?

Chapter 8
What's Next?

HOW DO I LIVE OUT THIS LIFE PROVIDED TO ME? HOW do I begin my new journey?

Pray for wisdom and for His will to be revealed to you, then all will be reset in your life.

> God gives wisdom, knowledge, and joy to those that please him. (Ecclesiastes: 2:26 NLT)

> Stick with wisdom and she will stick to you, protecting you throughout your days. She will rescue all those who passionately listen to her voice. Wisdom is the most valuable commodity—so buy it! Revelation knowledge is what you need—so invest in it! Wisdom will exalt you when you exalt her truth. She will lead you to honor and favor when you live your life by her insights. (Proverbs 4:6-8 TPT)

Use these steps on your path to a new future:

- Read your Bible. The Bible *IS* God's Word. It is called the "Living Word," as it speaks to you as you read it. The more you read, the more the veil is taken away and you will understand what your purpose is and how to achieve it.

- Pray. Pray all the time and commune with God like He is a friend. He loves us and is willing to help us if we ask Him and trust Him.

- Read books to continually renew your mind, and/or listen to audiobooks. I download an audio app and, since I have a pretty long drive in to work, I listen to that in the car. It makes the time go by fast and I don't get as angry and frustrated while driving anymore ☺.

- Get a daily journal book that has a Scripture verse and a short story for every day of the year. Do this in the morning and try to think on the Scripture all day long.

- Download a Bible app. There are many out there. I use #Bible and I set a time that I want it to send me one short verse each day. It takes just a few seconds to read them and then I am refreshed all over again!

- Give to the Lord. Many people think that the church just takes money and uses it for its own benefit. Some may, but many do not. Look for one that uses the funding wisely, for the purpose of filling God's kingdom. Then, give to that one. Or give to the less fortunate, or to an organization that helps people. Any way that you are led to give, do it, and do it with a happy heart. Give the FIRST ten percent of whatever it is that you make. You will not be disappointed in what God uses it for and how you are blessed in return.

Follow Proverbs 3:9-10: "Honor the lord with your wealth and with the best part of everything you produce. Then he will fill your barns with grain, and your vats will overflow with good wine." (NLT)

I started this many years ago and I am not rich by any means, but I always have what I need. My family never suffers,

and God always comes through and provides what we need—
sometimes right to the penny!

- Thank Him. Thank Him for what He has done in your
  life and what He will continue to do. He is the one who
  opens doors.

- Listen to worship music. Listen to it in the car, while
  cleaning the house, while taking a shower, and any
  other time you can find. It creates a spark into the
  heavenly realm like nothing else can.

- Get plugged in with other believers. If you don't
  already go to a good church, try some out and see what
  you like. There are all kinds, but you want one that
  speaks from the Bible, cares about people, and helps
  people get to know the Lord.

Listen to the voice of truth, and don't get caught up in the
matters of this world. Know that this is only temporary. You
CAN "Reset Your Life"! It is up to you to take the first step,
and then don't look back!